Connect

Workbook

Jack C. Richards
Carlos Barbisan
with Chuck Sandy
and Dorothy E. Zemach

CAMBRIDGE
UNIVERSITY PRESS

CAMBRIDGE UNIVERSITY PRESS
Cambridge, New York, Melbourne, Madrid, Cape Town, Singapore, São Paulo

Cambridge University Press
40 West 20th Street, New York, NY 10011–4211, USA
www.cambridge.org
Information on this title:www.cambridge.org/9780521594691 (English)
www.cambridge.org/9780521600644 (Portuguese)

© Cambridge University Press 2004

First published 2004
4th printing 2006

Printed in Hong Kong by Golden Cup Printing Co. Ltd.

ISBN-13 978-0-521-59470-7 Student's Book 4 (English)
ISBN-10 0-521-59470-7 Student's Book 4 (English)
ISBN-13 978-0-521-60071-2 Student's Book 4 (Portuguese)
ISBN-10 0-521-60071-5 Studen'ts Book 4 (Portuguese)
ISBN-13 978-0-521-59469-1 Workbook 4 (English)
ISBN-10 0-521-59469-3 Workbook 4 (English)
ISBN-13 978-0-521-60064-4 Workbook 4 (Portuguese)
ISBN-10 0-521-60064-2 Workbook 4 (Portuguese)
ISBN-13 978-0-521-59482-0 Teacher's Manual 4 (English)
ISBN-10 0-521-59468-4 Teacher's Manual 4 (English)
ISBN-13 978-0-521-59468-4 Teacher's Manual 4 (Portuguese)
ISBN-10 0-521-59468-5 Teacher's Manual 4 (Portuguese)
ISBN-13 978-0-521-59467-7 Class Audio Cassettes 4
ISBN-10 0-521-59467-7 Class Audio Cassettes 4
ISBN-13 978-0-521-59464-6 Class CD 4
ISBN-10 0-521-59464-2 Class CD 4

Art direction, book design, photo research, and layout services: Adventure House, NYC

Table of Contents

1 Last summer

1 **Complete the e-mail message with the correct form of the verbs in the box.**

☐ be ☐ buy ☐ have ☐ see ☐ watch
☐ break ☑ go ☐ play ☐ stay ☐ write

---
e-mail

Hi, Jeff,

What's up? Did you have a good summer vacation? You ___went___ mountain climbing, right? How _____ your trip? Please _____ me a message and tell me. I didn't go away this summer. I just _____ home. I _____ a lot of my friends, and we _____ videos. One day, while I _____ soccer, I _____ my watch. I _____ a new one the next day. I hope you _____ a great vacation. See you at school!

Your friend,
Chris

2 **Read the text. Then number the pictures in the correct order.**

I'm Kayley Stanton. I went to gymnastics camp with my friends last summer. We got up at 6:00 A.M. every day, but that was OK, because we also went to bed early. We were practicing gymnastics all the time. At the end of the summer, my best friend, Jenny, broke her finger when she was practicing some jumps. That was really too bad. We had a competition on the last day, and I won a prize! After camp was over, I had to do my summer homework. Now I'm back at school.

a. _____ b. _____ c. ___1___ d. _____ e. _____ f. _____

3 **Look at the information in part 2 again. Write questions and answers about Kayley.**

1. **Q:** _Where did Kayley go last summer?_ **A:** She went to gymnastics camp.

2. **Q:** Who did she go with? **A:** _____

3. **Q:** Were they practicing tennis all day? **A:** _____

4. **Q:** What time did they get up? **A:** _____

5. **Q:** _____ **A:** No, they didn't. They went to bed early.

6. **Q:** _____ **A:** She broke her finger.

Unit 1 My Life

Lesson 2 A new school year

1 Match the words in column A to the words in column B to make verb phrases. Then write the verb phrases.

Column A	Column B
1. join	fun
2. start	karate
3. have	Spanish
4. study	music lessons
5. do	a CD collection
6. take	the Art Club

1. *join the Art Club*
2. _____
3. _____
4. _____
5. _____
6. _____

2 Complete the conversations with the correct form of *would like to, want to, be going to,* or *have to.*

1. **A** Would you like to join the Chess Club?

   B Yes. *I'd like to* join the Chess Club. It sounds like fun!

2. **A** Do your sisters have to take a math class this year?

   B Yes, they do. _____ take math every year.

3. **A** Does Alberto have to study hard this year?

   B Yes. _____ study really hard! His parents want him to get better grades.

4. **A** Are they going to see the school play tonight?

   B No, they're not. _____ see the play tomorrow.

5. **A** Would your brother like to learn to speak German?

   B Yes. _____ learn German. It's a beautiful language.

6. **A** Do you want to visit the U.S. next year?

   B Yes, I do. _____ visit Los Angeles and Seattle.

3 Write sentences with your own information. Use the verb phrases in part 1 and *would like to* or *want to* for hopes and wishes, *be going to* for definite plans, and *have to* for obligations.

1. *I'd like to join the Art Club.*
2. _____
3. _____
4. _____
5. _____
6. _____

1 Write sentences about hopes and wishes, obligations, or definite plans.

1. **hope:** my best friend / join a new club
   My best friend wants to join a new club.
   OR *My best friend would like to join a new club.*

2. **wish:** Juanita / take piano lessons
   _____

3. **obligation:** my parents / take a trip this weekend
   _____

4. **definite plan:** Jorge and Jessica / go out tonight
   _____

5. **hope:** Carlos / get good grades this year
   _____

6. **definite plan:** my friends and I / go camping
   _____

7. **obligation:** you / get up early tomorrow
   _____

8. **wish:** Laura / stay out late tonight
   _____

9. **hope:** Keiko and Yuko / travel to Canada next year
   _____

10. **definite plan:** I / go to the movies on Saturday
   _____

2 Answer the questions with your own information.

1. What were you doing last Saturday at 10:00 A.M.? _____

2. What would you like to do tomorrow? _____

3. What were you doing last night at 7:00 P.M.? _____

4. What did you do last Saturday night? _____

5. What would you like to do in English class? _____

6. What subjects do you have to study next year? _____

7. What do you want to do in five years? _____

8. What are you going to do tomorrow? _____

Lesson 3 Life events

1 Write sentences in the simple past. Begin the appropriate sentences with *when*.

1. (Kenji / live in Argentina / learn Spanish)
   When *Kenji lived in Argentina, he* *learned Spanish* .

2. (Maria / make new friends / join the tennis team) _____

3. (Kim and Cody / learn to dance / take dance lessons) _____

4. (Nina / fall off her horse / break arm)
   When _____ .

5. (Paulo / go camping / lose his hat)
   When _____ .

6. (I / start high school / get a cell phone)
   When _____ .

2 Look at the time line below. Then write sentences about the events in Andy's life.

1. *When Andy was eight, he took acting lessons.* OR *Andy took acting lessons when he was eight.*

2. _____

3. _____

4. _____

5. _____

6. _____

7. _____

Then and now

1 Write sentences with *used to* and *not anymore.*

1. (Aria / shy) _Aria used to be shy, but she isn't anymore._

2. (I / like this song) _____

3. (Sandra / play the piano) _____

4. (I / take math) _____

5. (you / play computer games) _____

6. (Bill / stay up late) _____

7. (Keith and Marco / wear glasses) _____

8. (I / drink soda) _____

2 Look at the information about Marissa's life. Then write sentences about how her life has changed.

Before high school	Now
took easy classes	takes difficult classes
had lots of free time after school	has no free time
knew just a few people	knows many people
had a radio	has a CD player
listened to country music	listens to rock music
read comic books	reads mystery stories
stayed home on weekends	goes camping on weekends

1. _Marissa used to take easy classes, but she doesn't_
   anymore. Now she takes difficult classes.

2. _____

3. _____

4. _____

5. _____

6. _____

7. _____

Lesson 5 Connections

1 Complete the sentences with the simple past or the past continuous form of the verbs.

1. Peter _____broke_____ (break) his glasses when he __was playing__ (play) tennis.

2. When Kim _____ (join) the soccer team, she _____ (meet) her friend, Lisa.

3. My friend _____ (fall) when he _____ (dance).

4. When Chris _____ (be) nine years old, he _____ (learn) to surf.

5. My family and I _____ (eat) dinner when you _____ (call).

6. I _____ (be) scared when I _____ (watch) that movie!

7. Melissa _____ (get) an award when she _____ (win) the competition.

8. When class _____ (start), Julio and Raul _____ (play) a game.

2 Read the text about Sofia. Then write about how her life has changed. Use *used to* and *not anymore*.

Hi! I'm Sofia. When I was younger, I lived in Mexico City. I spoke only Spanish and ate only Mexican food. I learned some traditional Mexican folk dances, too. My family moved to New York when I was 12. We spoke only English and ate only American food. I took ballet lessons in school. And now? I live in Chicago. When I moved here, I got a job as a teacher. I don't teach now. I work for a big company. I don't take ballet lessons, but I'm taking a salsa class. It's great!

1. (live in Mexico) *Sofia used to live in Mexico, but she doesn't anymore.*

2. (speak only Spanish) _____

3. (eat only Mexican food) _____

4. (live in New York) _____

5. (take ballet lessons) _____

3 Write sentences about Sofia. Begin the appropriate sentences with *when*.

1. (graduate from high school / be 18) *Sofia graduated from high school when she was 18.*

2. (live in an apartment / move to Chicago) _____

3. (22 / move to Chicago) _____

4. (live in Mexico City / be younger) When _____ .

5. (take ballet lessons / hurt her foot) When _____ .

6. (have American friends / live in New York) _____

7. (be a teacher / teach Spanish) When _____ .

8. (not eat Mexican food / live in New York) _____

6 Predictions

1 Cara was born in April. Read the predictions for this year for people born in April. Then answer the questions.

> *Were you born in April?* You won't have much money this year, so don't buy too many things! You'll take a few short trips this year, but you won't take a long trip. You'll have a fight with your best friend in May. Don't worry – you'll be friends again in June!

1. Will Cara buy a lot of things? *No, she won't.*

2. Will she take any long trips this year? _____

3. Will she have a fight with a friend? _____

4. Will she have a lot of money this year? _____

5. Will she take any short trips this year? _____

2 Write questions with the verb phrases in the box.

☐ buy the shirt ☐ cook dinner ☑ miss the bus
☐ catch the ball ☐ go to the library ☐ see a movie

1. **Q:** *Will they miss the bus?*
   A: No, they won't.

2. **Q:** _____
   A: Yes, he will.

3. **Q:** _____
   A: Yes, they will.

4. **Q:** _____
   A: No, he won't.

5. **Q:** _____
   A: No, I won't.

6. **Q:** _____
   A: Yes, she will.

3 Toshi is thinking about the future. Write sentences about his predictions. Use *will* or *won't*.

In the future . . .

1. (animals / talk) *Animals will talk.* _____

2. (people / go on vacations in outer space) _____

3. (people / not get sick) _____

4. (space aliens / visit Earth) _____

5. (men / not wear ties) _____

Lesson 7 When I'm older

1 Complete the conversation with the sentences in the box.

> ☐ No. She probably won't go to college until next year.   ☐ She'll probably work for our father in his office.
> ☐ No. She probably won't go to Europe.   ☐ She probably will.
> ☐ No, she won't. She'll probably travel with her friends.   ☐ She probably won't.
> ☑ She'll probably take a trip.

Kim Your sister's graduating from high school this year, right? What's she going to do?

Greg I'm not sure. *She'll probably take a trip.* She wants to relax after she graduates.

Kim Where will she go? Europe?

Greg _____ She doesn't have a lot of money.

Kim Will she travel alone?

Greg _____

Kim And after that? Will she go to college?

Greg _____ She needs to earn some money before she goes to college.

Kim So, what will she do this year?

Greg _____ He needs help.

Kim Maybe someday she'll get a great job!

Greg _____ She's smart. But she'll have to finish college first.

Kim If she lives at home for another year, she can help you with your Spanish homework.

Greg _____ She says I have to learn Spanish by myself.

Kim Then we can work together. I have to study Spanish this year, too!

2 Make verb phrases with the words below and the words in the box. Then make predictions about yourself. Use *will probably* or *probably won't*.

> be   get   go

1. famous	*be famous*	*I probably won't be famous.*
2. a driver's license		
3. to college		
4. rich		
5. a job		
6. an actor		
7. a pet		
8. married		

Mini-review

1 Complete the text with the correct form of *want to*, *will*, or *won't*.

I _want to_ travel to South America. I probably _____ visit all the countries, but I _____ definitely visit most of them. I'd like to go camping most of the time, so I probably _____ visit a lot of cities. I _____ see the rain forest, so I _____ go hiking through the jungle or take a boat trip. I _____ probably see a lot of animals. I _____ bring my camera, but I probably _____ take very good pictures. I'm a terrible photographer!

2 Unscramble the questions. Then write answers with *will, won't, will probably*, or *probably won't* and your own information.

1. Will / math teacher / week / this / give / test / a / your ?

   Q: _Will your math teacher give a test this week?_

   A: _No, he probably won't._

2. a / take / family / your / Will / this / year / vacation ?

   Q: _____

   A: _____

3. favorite / Will / your / record / CD / singer / year / this / a ?

   Q: _____

   A: _____

4. early / bed / go / tonight / you / Will / to ?

   Q: _____

   A: _____

5. new / computer / buy / you / month / next / a / Will ?

   Q: _____

   A: _____

6. best friend / to / Will / Venezuela / travel / summer / this / your ?

   Q: _____

   A: _____

7. you / a / Will / go / December / to / party / in ?

   Q: _____

   A: _____

8. classmates / college / your / Will / to / go / year / next ?

   Q: _____

   A: _____

Lesson 8 Teen Center

1 Complete the sentences with the words in the box.
Then complete the puzzle.

☑ activity ☐ edit ☐ learn ☐ model ☐ record
☐ articles ☐ join ☐ martial ☐ Racket ☐ take

Down

1. Ballroom dancing is my favorite after-school _activity_ .

2. Learn how to _____ your own CD in this exciting class.

4. To learn salsa, _____ a dance class!

5. Join the _____ Club and play tennis.

6. Karate is a type of _____ art.

9. Do you want to _____ how to make a scrapbook?

Across

3. This year I'm going to _____ the Photography Club.

7. A reporter writes _____ for the newspaper.

8. An art _____ has to sit still.

10. After you make your music video, you might need to _____ it.

2 Write sentences with *might* or *might not*.

1. Kelly loves to draw, but she's very busy this semester.

   (art classes) _She might not take art classes this semester._

2. Sam and Max like to try new foods.

   (cooking class) _____

3. Jason and I aren't good writers.

   (reporters) _____

4. I play the trumpet.

   (marching band) _____

5. Karen loves art, but she can't sit still for a long time.

   (art model) _____

6. Sheila isn't good at badminton.

   (Racket Club) _____

7. John and Dave watch a lot of karate movies.

   (martial arts classes) _____

Lesson 9 After high school

1 Look at Serena's and Leo's plans for the future. Then write sentences with *be going to, will, will probably, probably won't,* or *might.*

> ✓ = a definite plan   O = a probable plan   ? = a possible plan

Serena

✓ go to college
✓ find an apartment in the city
O visit my grandparents
O not take violin lessons
? take a dance class

Leo

O take a vacation
✓ get a job
? take a computer class
O not go on a group tour
? travel alone

1. *She's going to go to college.*
2. _____
3. _____
4. _____
5. _____

6. _____
7. _____
8. _____
9. _____
10. _____

2 Write sentences about your future plans and the plans of people you know.

1. **definite plan:** (my family)

   My family will travel to Puerto Rico this summer.

   OR *My family is going to travel to Puerto Rico this summer.*

2. **probable plan:** (my friend)

   _____

3. **possible plan:** (my English teacher)

   _____

4. **probable plan:** (my classmates)

   _____

5. **definite plan:** (I)

   _____

6. **possible plan:** (my favorite sports team)

   _____

Lesson 10 Connections

1 Which after-school activities will Lisa choose? Look at her answers to the personality survey in the school newspaper. Then write sentences with *will probably, probably won't, might,* or *might not*.

Personality Survey What should you try? Take this survey to find out!	a lot	a little	not at all
1. Do you like to cook?	☐	☑	☐
2. Do you like languages?	☐	☑	☐
3. Do you like team sports?	☐	☐	☑
4. Do you like to play any musical instruments?	☑	☐	☐
5. Do you like computers?	☐	☐	☑
6. Do you like to dance?	☑	☐	☐
7. Do you like to read?	☐	☑	☐
8. Do you like to write articles?	☑	☐	☐
9. Do you like to play tennis?	☐	☑	☐
10. Do you like to do karate?	☐	☐	☑

1. (cooking class) *Lisa might take a cooking class.*

   OR *Lisa might not take a cooking class.*

2. (French Club) _____

3. (volleyball team) _____

4. (marching band) _____

5. (Computer Club) _____

6. (ballroom dancing class) _____

7. (Book Club) _____

8. (reporter for school newspaper) _____

9. (Racket Club) _____

10. (Martial Arts Club) _____

2 Write the names of people below. Then write three predictions about them. Write about what they *will probably, probably won't,* and *might* be doing in the next five years.

a) two classmates: _____

   They'll probably travel abroad.

1. _____

2. _____

3. _____

b) a friend: _____

4. _____

5. _____

6. _____

c) a family member: _____

7. _____

8. _____

9. _____

d) an actor or a singer: _____

10. _____

11. _____

12. _____

11 Weekend plans

1 Complete the conversations. Accept or refuse the invitations.

1. **A** Would you like to play tennis with me?

   B _Sure, I'd love to._____ I'll get my racket!

2. **A** Would you like to go to the park on Saturday?

   B _____ I'm going to my cousin's house on Saturday.

3. **A** Would you like to go swimming with me this afternoon?

   B _____ I have to go to soccer practice.

4. **A** Would you like to go to a movie this weekend?

   B _____ Let's see a comedy!

5. **A** Would you like to come over this weekend?

   B _____ I'm going camping with my family.

6. **A** Would you like to take a dance class with me?

   B _____ How about a ballroom dancing class?

2 Write invitations with *Would you like to*.

1. (watch *The Matrix*)

   Q: _Would you like to watch The Matrix?_____

   A: Sure, I'd love to. *The Matrix* is one of my favorite movies.

2. (go skiing on Saturday)

   Q: _____

   A: I'm sorry, but I can't. I don't know how to ski!

3. (go to a magic show)

   Q: _____

   A: Yes, I'd love to. I really like magic shows.

4. (drive go-carts)

   Q: _____

   A: Sure, I'd like to. We can race each other!

5. (play soccer this weekend)

   Q: _____

   A: I'm sorry, but I can't. Can we play next weekend?

6. (have lunch)

   Q: _____

   A: I'd love to, but I can't. I have a Chess Club meeting at lunchtime.

Unit 3 Plans

Lesson 12 Evening plans

1 Complete the conversations with the sentences in the box.

> ☐ Absolutely not! You can't drive.   ☐ Sure. But please be careful with it.
> ☐ No, I'm sorry. My back hurts.   ☐ Sure. I'll call you at 7:00.
> ☐ No, I'm sorry. I'll be home late.   ☑ Yes, of course. I'm good at math.

1. **A** Could you help me with my math homework?

   B *Yes, of course. I'm good at math.*

2. **A** Could you help me move this table?

   B _____

3. **A** Can I try your digital camera?

   B _____

4. **A** Can I borrow your car tonight, Dad?

   B _____

5. **A** Can I come over after school?

   B _____

6. **A** Could you call me later?

   B _____

2 Write questions to ask for permission or to make a request.

1. (I / use / eraser) *Can I use your eraser?* _____

2. (I / borrow / money for lunch) _____

3. (you / explain / this math problem) _____

4. (you / open / the window) _____

3 Look at part 2 again. Answer the questions.

1. (yes) *Sure, that's fine.*   3. (yes) _____

2. (yes) _____   4. (no) _____

Plans 15

1 Complete the conversations with *can, could,* or *would.*

1. **A** Hi, Ellen. _Would_ you like to do something with me this weekend?

   B Sure, I'd like to. _____ you call me after school? We can make plans then.

2. **A** _____ I use your new game?

   B Yes. It's a lot of fun. You'll enjoy it.

3. **A** _____ you help me do research for my report?

   B Yes, of course. _____ you like to meet tonight?

4. **A** _____ you like to go to a movie tonight?

   B Sure, but _____ you lend me some money? I don't have any!

5. **A** Hey, _____ you like to listen to my new CD?

   B Sorry. I have to get to class. _____ I listen to it later?

6. **A** _____ I go to Dave's party this weekend, Mom?

   B Yes, all right. But _____ you clean your room first?

2 Write questions with *would you like to, could you,* or *can I.*
Then answer the questions with your own information.

1. (you / sleep / tent)

   Q: _Would you like to sleep in a tent?_

   A: _____

2. (you / lend / your notebook)

   Q: _____

   A: _____

3. (you / explore / rain forest)

   Q: _____

   A: _____

4. (I / stay out late / tonight)

   Q: _____

   A: _____

5. (you / clean / the cafeteria)

   Q: _____

   A: _____

6. (I / borrow / your cell phone)

   Q: _____

   A: _____

13 Making plans

1 Complete the sentences with the clauses in the box.

> ☐ Danny might lend you some money   ☐ My family will probably move
> ☑ he'll probably help make dinner   ☐ my friends might have a barbecue
> ☐ I might ask him to help me with my homework   ☐ she'll probably miss the show
> ☐ I won't watch the horror movie   ☐ We'll take the bus

1. If my father comes home early, *he'll probably help make dinner* .

2. _____ if it's too scary.

3. If the weather is nice this weekend, _____ .

4. _____ if you ask him.

5. If Giovanni is finished with his homework, _____ .

6. _____ if we find a larger house.

7. If Carla is late, _____ .

8. _____ if we go downtown.

2 Answer the questions in two different ways. Use *if* and your own information.

1. What will you eat for lunch today?
   (will: very hungry / not very hungry) *If I'm very hungry, I'll eat a sandwich,*

   some fruit, and a cookie. If I'm not very hungry, I'll eat two apples.

2. What will you do this weekend?
   (might: rains / doesn't rain) _____

3. What will you do tonight?
   (will probably: have homework / don't have homework) _____

4. What movie will you see?
   (won't: see a comedy / see an action movie) _____

5. What will you buy at your favorite store?
   (might: a lot of money / a little money) _____

6. What will you do after school today?
   (will: tired / not tired) _____

Lesson 14 Vacation plans

1 Complete these instructions for using a new computer printer with *before*, *while*, and *after*.

1. Read the instructions _before_ you take the printer out of the box.

2. _____ you take the printer out of the box, put it on the table.

3. _____ you turn on the computer, connect it to the printer.

4. Turn on the printer _____ you turn on the computer.

5. Make sure you add paper _____ you try to print!

6. And remember – never eat or drink _____ you are near your printer.

2 Write sentences with *before*, *while*, or *after*.

1. he / going to go swimming / school

   (after) _He's going to go swimming after school._

2. close the door / you come in

   (after) _____

3. she / can't talk on the phone / doing homework

   (while) _____

4. Gino and Marie / have to study / the big test

   (before)_____

3 Write sentences with your own information.

1. (before I go to bed) _Before I go to bed, I might read a book._ OR _I might read a book_

   before I go to bed.

2. (after I finish this Workbook page) _____

3. (while I'm in school next week) _____

4. (after I finish high school) _____

Lesson 15 Connections

1 Look at Selina's list. Then write sentences about the things she will do before, during, and after her vacation in the country.

	Things to do before I leave	Things to do while I'm on vacation	Things to do after I get back
	• buy horseback-riding gear	• go hiking	• get some rest
	• finish schoolwork	• take horseback-riding lessons	• wash clothes
	• borrow Kay's digital camera	• write postcards	• call friends

1. _She'll buy horseback-riding gear before she leaves._
2. _____
3. _____
4. _____
5. _____
6. _____
7. _____
8. _____
9. _____

2 What will Selina do if these things happen? Write sentences with *will*, *won't*, or *might*.

1. won't: can't buy horseback-riding gear / take horseback-riding lessons
   If she can't buy horseback-riding gear, she won't take horseback-riding lessons.

2. might: Kay's camera doesn't work / borrow Marty's camera
   _____

3. won't: weather is bad / go hiking
   _____

4. might: horseback-riding lessons too expensive / take a long walk
   _____

5. won't: doesn't have time / write postcards
   _____

6. will: too exhausted / wash clothes later
   _____

16 Teens online

1 Complete the answers with the gerund form of the verb phrases in the box.

> ☐ (Chat) online is one of my favorite activities. ☐ (Listen) to music is great!
> ☐ (Find) information online takes a long time. ☑ (Play) computer games is boring.
> ☐ (Go) to the beach is nice when it's hot. ☐ (Play) racket sports isn't fun for me.

1. **Q:** Do you like computer games?   **A:** No, I don't. *Playing computer games is boring.*

2. **Q:** Do you like music?   **A:** Yes, I do. _____

3. **Q:** Do you play racket sports?   **A:** No, I don't. _____

4. **Q:** Do you go to the beach in the summer?   **A:** Yes, I do. _____

5. **Q:** Do you chat online?   **A:** Yes, I do. _____

6. **Q:** Do you find information online?   **A:** No, I don't. _____

2 Answer the questions in part 1 with your own information.

1. _____
2. _____
3. _____
4. _____
5. _____
6. _____

3 Write answers. Use short answers and gerunds as objects.

1. **Q:** Does Jenny like to ski?
   A: (yes) *Yes, she does. She likes skiing.* _____

2. **Q:** Does Paul like to dance?
   A: (no) _____

3. **Q:** Do your parents like to use e-mail?
   A: (yes) _____

4. **Q:** Does Ms. Hill like to do crossword puzzles?
   A: (yes) _____

5. **Q:** Do your sisters like to do chores?
   A: (no) _____

6. **Q:** Does your father like to play video games?
   A: (no) _____

7. **Q:** Do your friends like to watch action movies?
   A: (yes) _____

Lesson 17 Personality types

1 Complete the puzzle. Then write the letters in each [ ] in the puzzle to form a popular personality type.

☐ bad-tempered	☑ forgetful	☐ independent	☐ thoughtful
☐ creative	☐ hardworking	☐ organized	☐ trustworthy

1. Someone who doesn't remember things is _____ .

2. A _____ person might be good at art or music.

3. If the things in your room aren't in order, you should be more _____ !

4. Don't get angry too often. No one likes a _____ friend!

5. Someone who is _____ does a lot of things without help.

6. Students who are _____ often get good grades.

7. A _____ person does nice things for friends.

8. Your parents want you to be _____ and honest.

```
                              1.[f]o r g e t f u l
                          2. _ [_] _ _ _ _ _ _ _
                      3. _ _ _ _ _ [_] _ _ _
                  4.   _ _ _ - [_] _ _ _ _ _ _
                5. _ _ _ _ _ _ _ [_] _ _
              6.   _ _ _ [_] _ _ _
          7.   _ _ _ _ _ _ _ _ [_]
        8.   _ _ _ _ _ _ _ _ _ _ [_]

A popular personality type is _____ .
```

2 How are these people similar? Write sentences.

1. Sebastian is outgoing. (Mei Mei and Tamia) *Mei Mei and Tamia are, too.*

2. Carrie is creative. (her brother) _____

3. My mother doesn't want help doing things. (my father) _____

4. I'm not athletic. (my cousins) _____

5. Kenji studies hard. (Aya and Miho) _____

6. Sue doesn't like going out alone. (her friends) _____

7. I make friends easily. (my sister) _____

8. Selma isn't forgetful. (Wayne) _____

1 Complete the questions with gerunds as objects.

1. **Q:** Do you like *going to the beach* _____ ?

   A: No, I don't. I can't swim, and I don't know how to surf or water-ski.

2. **Q:** Do you like _____ ?

   A: Yes, I do. Crossword puzzles are great!

3. **Q:** Do you enjoy _____ ?

   A: No, I don't. I don't know how to play chess!

4. **Q:** Do you like _____ ?

   A: Yes, I do. I go to the library every week.

5. **Q:** Do you enjoy _____ ?

   A: No, I don't. But my parents always have a lot of things for me to do, like washing the dishes.

6. **Q:** Do you enjoy _____ ?

   A: Yes, I do. My friends play games online, too.

2 Read Simon's information. Write about his likes, dislikes, and personality. Then write sentences agreeing with Simon's preferences and personality.

Simon

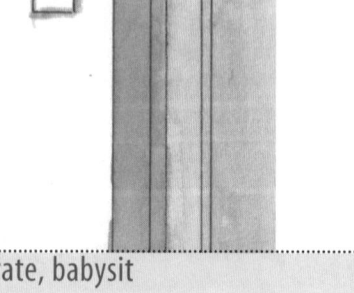

Likes: do karate, babysit
Dislikes: play baseball, listen to classical music
Personality: thoughtful, outgoing

1. *Simon likes doing karate.*   *I do, too. Doing karate is fun!*

2. _____ _____

3. _____ _____

4. _____ _____

5. _____ _____

6. _____ _____

Lesson 18 Unusual people

1 Look at the information. Then write sentences.

1. have / history teacher / collects cars

I have a history teacher who collects cars.

2. know / brother and sister / surf in competitions

_____

_____

3. met / swimmer / an Olympic champion

_____

_____

4. met / teen / collect spiders

_____

_____

5. have / friend / good at English

_____

_____

6. know / woman / goes camping in the snow

_____

_____

2 Read Hannah's description of people in her high school. Then write sentences about the people she knew.

When I was in high school, I knew some people with unusual hobbies. For example, Mike collected chess pieces – and he didn't even play chess! My best friend, Katrina, loved animals. She went to the zoo every day after school. A girl in my science class painted pictures of insects. Another girl in the same class watched old movies every weekend. Two boys in my English class liked to go hiking in the rain. The basketball coach, Miss Thomas, liked to tell fortunes. My math teacher, Mr. Marks, read poetry in cafés at night, and Ms. Spencer, the librarian, made all her own clothes. It was an interesting school!

1. *Hannah knew a girl who painted pictures of insects.*

2. _____

3. _____

4. _____

5. _____

6. _____

7. _____

8. _____

Lesson 19 — Who's that girl?

1 Complete the conversation with tag questions.

Cristina Hi. You're new at this school, _aren't you_ ?

Anita Yes, I am. You're in my English class, _____?

Cristina Yes, I sit behind you. It's a good class, _____?

Anita Yes, I think so. But the new unit is hard, _____?

Cristina Oh, it's not too bad. Would you like some help?

Anita Sure, that would be great. You're good at English, _____?
Actually, you do well in all your classes, _____?

Cristina No, I don't! I'm terrible at math. But you like math, _____?

Anita Not really. Why do you think so?

Cristina Well, you're carrying your math book, _____?

Anita Yes, I am. We have homework tonight, _____?

Cristina Yes! I forgot!

2 Write tag questions and answers.

1. Tom / be good at math

   Q: _Tom is good at math, isn't he?_

   A: _Yes, he is._

2. Gina / like dogs

   Q: _____

   A: _____

3. your cousins / live in the country

   Q: _____

   A: _____

4. those mountains / be very big

   Q: _____

   A: _____

5. you / like music

   Q: _____

   A: _____

6. Manuel / play the piano

   Q: _____

   A: _____

Lesson 20 Connections

1 **Write tag questions and answers.**

1. Yao Ming / basketball player

   Q: *Yao Ming is a basketball player, isn't he?* **A:** *Yes, he is.*

2. the Rolling Stones / play classical music

   Q: _____ **A:** _____

3. Shakira / sing in French

   Q: _____ **A:** _____

4. soccer / be racket sport

   Q: _____ **A:** _____

5. people / speak Spanish in Colombia

   Q: _____ **A:** _____

6. the Dixie Chicks / like singing

   Q: _____ **A:** _____

2 **Look at Eva's photo album. Then write sentences about the people she knows.**

Ms. Allen, my teacher, lives in the city.

My friends, Tony and Hector, play on the soccer team.

Carolina, my best friend, loves horseback riding.

My computer partner, Victor, is a reporter for the school newspaper.

Victoria, my e-pal, writes e-mail messages every day.

Mr. Campbell, my tennis coach, rides a motorcycle.

1. *She has a teacher who lives in the city.* _____

2. _____

3. _____

4. _____

5. _____

6. _____

People 25

For fun

1 **Write the present perfect form of the verb.**

1. be _have been_
2. call _____
3. clean _____
4. do _____
5. eat _____

6. go _____
7. hang out _____
8. have _____
9. make _____
10. play _____

11. read _____
12. rent _____
13. see _____
14. study _____
15. watch _____

2 **Complete the text with the present perfect.**

My best friend and I _____ (do) a lot of fun things this year.

We _____ (watch) six soccer matches, we _____ (go)

to 12 movies, and we _____ (hang) out at the beach every weekend.

I _____ (not do) all of my homework, and I _____ (not clean)

my room. My parents aren't happy, but I am!

3 **Beatriz and Ana are planning a party. Look at their list. Then write
sentences about the things they have done (✓) and the things they
haven't done (✗).**

TO DO

✗ rent videos
✓ invite friends
✓ clean the kitchen
✗ clean the living room
✓ make the decorations
✗ go to the store
✓ make a cake
✗ finish all our chores

1. _We haven't rented videos._ _____
2. _____
3. _____
4. _____
5. _____
6. _____
7. _____
8. _____

4 **Write about what you have and haven't done.**

1. (exercise today) _____
2. (read the newspaper today) _____
3. (watch TV this week) _____
4. (see a movie this week) _____
5. (go to the mountains this year) _____
6. (do my homework today) _____
7. (do chores this week) _____
8. (go shopping this month) _____

Unit 5 Entertainment

22 Young entertainers

1 Complete the verb phrases with the words in the box.

☐ entertain   ☐ give   ☐ record   ☐ sign   ☑ star   ☐ support

1. ___star___ in a movie
2. _____ interviews
3. _____ a song

4. _____ autographs
5. _____ a charity
6. _____ a live audience

2 What have these entertainers done? What haven't they done? Look at the pictures. Then write sentences with the verb phrases in part 1.

Manuel

The Chicklets

1. _Manuel has supported a charity._
2. _____
3. _____

4. _____
5. _____
6. _____

3 Look at the pictures. Then correct the false information. Use the present perfect.

Ayako / record two CDs

1. _Ayako hasn't recorded two CDs. She's_
recorded three CDs.

the Eagles / win soccer games

2. _____

_____

Silvio / appear on TV

3. _____

_____

Ginny / travel to New Zealand

4. _____

_____

Mini-review

1 Complete the sentences with the present perfect form of the verb phrases in the box.

☐ appear in the school newspaper   ☑ meet a lot of artists
☐ give interviews   ☐ record one song
☐ have too much homework   ☐ win an Academy Award
☐ make a movie   ☐ win any games

1. I'm a photographer. I go to a lot of parties, and I *have met a lot of artists* .

2. That new singer, Andreas, _____ .
   He wants to record a whole CD next year.

3. Beyoncé is my favorite singer and actress. She
   _____ , but she has won many Grammy Awards!

4. My friend wants to be a filmmaker. He _____ ,
   but he's edited a movie.

5. They are very popular. They _____
   to every news show on TV!

6. My picture hasn't been in any fashion magazines, but I
   _____ twice.

7. Iliana hasn't had time to hang out this week.
   She _____ .

8. The school basketball team has practiced a lot this year,
   but they _____ .

2 Complete the sentences about Cheryl. Use the present perfect. Then
write sentences about yourself and people you know.

1. Cheryl *has been* (be) busy this week.
   I've been busy this week, too. OR *I haven't been busy this week.*

2. Cheryl's friends _____ (have) a lot of homework.

   _____

3. She _____ (see) some good TV shows today.

   _____

4. Cheryl's family _____ (not eat) dinner together this week.

   _____

5. She _____ (not go) to the mall this month.

   _____

6. Cheryl _____ (read) the newspaper every day this week.

   _____

23 Are you a fan?

1 Complete the conversation. Write present perfect questions with *ever,* and answer the questions.

Renaldo I'm having trouble with my English composition. We have to write about our lives. But I've had a very boring life!

Joe No, you haven't! Let's think. (try / any dangerous sports?)
Have you ever tried any dangerous sports?

Renaldo (No) *No, I haven't.* I'm not very athletic.

Joe (meet / movie star?) _____

Renaldo (No) _____ I'm not interested in movies. I like music.

Joe OK! (go / any concerts?) _____

Renaldo (Yes) _____ My friends and I have gone to a few concerts.

Joe (be invited / backstage?) _____

Renaldo (Yes) _____ We've been invited backstage a few times. It was fun.

Joe Wow! (get / any autographs?) _____

Renaldo (No) _____ But maybe next time!

Joe Maybe! And you have something to write about now.

2 Answer the questions.

1. **Q:** Have you ever written a fan letter?
   A: *Yes, I have.* I wrote a fan letter to David Beckham.

2. **Q:** Have your friends ever won tickets to a concert?
   A: _____ They never win contests!

3. **Q:** Has your mother ever gone to a concert?
   A: _____ She went to a lot of concerts when she was younger.

4. **Q:** Have your friends ever given you presents?
   A: _____ They give me presents every year for my birthday.

5. **Q:** Have you ever tried water-skiing?
   A: _____ I don't like water sports.

6. **Q:** Has your best friend ever helped you with your homework?
   A: _____ He helps me every day.

3 Answer the questions with your own information.

1. Have you ever been interviewed? _____

2. Has your best friend ever appeared on TV? _____

3. Has your school ever been in the newspaper? _____

4. Has your favorite singer ever won an award? _____

5. Have you ever traveled to another city? _____

6. Have you ever gotten a star's autograph? _____

Pop culture trivia

1 Write questions and answers.

1. (Keanu Reeves / be an actor) *How long has Keanu Reeves been an actor?*
   (he was in high school) *He's been an actor since he was in high school.*

2. (Tiger Woods / play professional golf) _____
   (1996) _____

3. (J.K. Rowling / write *Harry Potter* books) _____
   (about ten years) _____

4. (the Olsen twins / be actors) _____
   (more than 15 years) _____

5. (Angelina Jolie / acted in movies) _____
   (1982) _____

6. (Linkin Park / be a rock group) _____
   (a few years) _____

7. (you watch / reality shows on TV) _____
   (four years) _____

8. (Jennifer Aniston / be married to Brad Pitt) _____
   (2000) _____

2 Look at the chart. Write questions and answers about Elias.

> played the guitar – since he was 11
> written music – 1995
> lived in Los Angeles – 5 years
> worked as a musician – 3 years
> played in a band – 2003

1. **Q:** *How long has Elias played the guitar?*
   A: *He's played the guitar since he was 11.*

2. **Q:** _____
   A: _____

3. **Q:** _____
   A: _____

4. **Q:** _____
   A: _____

5. **Q:** _____
   A: _____

Lesson 25 Connections

1 Write the present perfect form of the verbs.

1. become   *has become*
2. buy   _____
3. celebrate   _____
4. change   _____
5. get   _____
6. give   _____
7. meet   _____

8. receive   _____
9. record   _____
10. show   _____
11. sing   _____
12. take   _____
13. try   _____
14. write   _____

2 Complete the article about Emma Watson with *for* or *since*.

I've been an Emma Watson fan *for* more than five years. Here's some information about her:

Emma Watson plays Hermione Granger in the *Harry Potter* movies. She was born in France in 1990, but she has lived in England _____ she was 5. She's been an actress _____ a long time. She has acted in plays _____ she was in elementary school. She hasn't won any prizes for acting, but she has won a competition. She won first prize in a poetry competition when she was 7. She has enjoyed reading _____ many years, so it's no surprise that she acts in movies that come from books. She has acted in the *Harry Potter* movies _____ 2001. Emma loves animals and has had two cats _____ many years.

3 Complete the questions about Emma Watson with *Has she ever* or *How long has she*. Then write answers.

1. *How long has she* been an actress? *She's been an actress for a long time.*
2. _____ acted in plays? _____
3. _____ won an acting prize? _____
4. _____ won a competition? _____
5. _____ acted in the *Harry Potter* movies? _____
6. _____ been to France? _____
7. _____ lived in England? _____

4 Answer the questions with your own information.

1. How long have you studied English? _____
2. Have you ever visited Argentina? _____
3. How long have you lived in your town? _____
4. Have you ever lived in another town? _____

Entertainment 31

1 Make verb phrases with the words below and the verbs in the box.
Then write sentences with the verb phrases and your own information.

☐ dye ☐ get ☐ go out ☐ start
☐ explore ☑ go ☐ sing ☐ try

1. skydiving — _go skydiving_ — _I've never gone skydiving._

2. my hair

3. a band

4. a cave

5. a tattoo

6. new food

7. karaoke

8. without permission

2 The Mendoza family has not done any of these things.
Write questions and answers.

1. **Q:** Have Mr. and Mrs. Mendoza ever been in a sports competition?
   A: _No, they haven't. They've never been in a sports competition._ OR _No, never._

2. **Q:** ____
   A: No, she hasn't. She's never gone horseback riding.

3. **Q:** ____
   A: No, they haven't. Emilio and Ella have never sung karaoke.

4. **Q:** Have the Mendozas ever gone hiking in the jungle?
   A: ____

5. **Q:** Has Emilio ever acted in a play?
   A: ____

6. **Q:** Has Max ever gone camping with the family?
   A: ____

Lesson 27 What we've done

1 Complete the sentences with *ago, for, since,* or *so far.*

1. I've liked classical music *for* many years.
2. She hasn't read comic books _____ she was a child.
3. Our volleyball team has done really well _____ .
4. I've studied English _____ five years.
5. Enrique met his new teacher a week _____ .
6. Carlo hasn't scored a goal in this game _____ .
7. I went to Puerto Rico with my family two months _____ .
8. I haven't gotten any e-mail messages _____ Friday.

2 Complete the conversation with the simple past or the present perfect.

Josh Hi, Emily. Where *have you been* (you / be)? _____ (I / not see) you for a long time.

Emily I know. _____ (I / be) in Dallas with my cousins. _____ (I / come back) a week ago.

Josh What _____ (you / do) there?

Emily _____ (I / go) horseback riding every day. _____ (My cousins / have) their own horses since _____ (they / be) little kids.

Josh Do you like horseback riding? Did you fall off the horse?

Emily I love it, and _____ (I / not fall off) at all! Actually, I think horseback riding is the best thing _____ (I / do) so far this year.

3 Answer the questions with your own information.

1. What's something you've done since you were a small child?

   _____

2. What did you do last weekend?

   _____

3. What have you done since last summer?

   _____

4. What holiday or event has your family celebrated for many years?

   _____

5. What's something that you started to do this year?

   _____

6. What's the most interesting thing you've learned so far this year?

   _____

Mini-review

1 Choose the correct word to complete the sentences.

1. Have you _ever_ (ever / never) tried Indian food?

2. Two of my friends _____ (have gone / went) skydiving last week.

3. I've had a lot of interesting experiences _____ (for / since) last year.

4. My father ran a marathon two months _____ (ago / since).

5. _____ (Did you have / Have you had) a good time yesterday?

6. Cindy has _____ (ever / never) played with a rock band.

7. Ken hasn't won any prizes _____ (since / so far).

8. I haven't seen my best friend _____ (for / since) two weeks.

2 Look at the information. Then write questions and long answers about Adelina.

Adelina
1. have a pet → since she was five
2. meet a rock star → never
3. sail a boat → two weeks ago
4. be an art model → for a long time
5. run a marathon → last year
6. write e-mail messages in English → never

1. **Q:** _Has Adelina ever had a pet?_
   A: _Yes, she has. She's had a pet since she was five._

2. **Q:** _____
   A: _____

3. **Q:** _____
   A: _____

4. **Q:** _____
   A: _____

5. **Q:** _____
   A: _____

6. **Q:** _____
   A: _____

Lesson 28 Amazing teens

1 Fidel and Paco are traveling around Australia. Write sentences about what they have already done and what they have not done yet.

1. _They've already hiked in the rain forest._

2. _____

3. _____

4. _____

5. _____

6. _____

7. _____

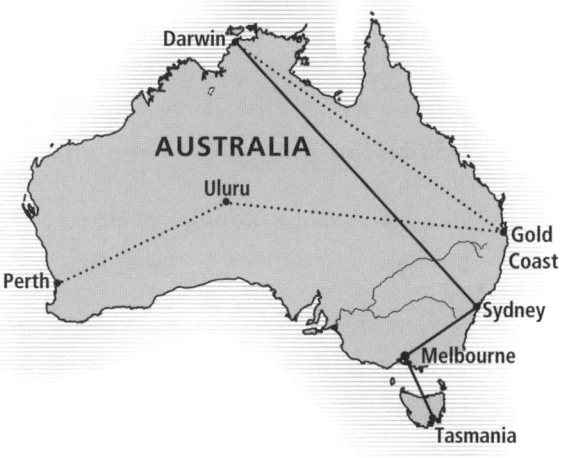

THINGS TO DO IN AUSTRALIA

- ☑ Tasmania: hike in rain forest
- ☑ Melbourne: go to a rock concert
- ☑ Sydney: see the Sydney Opera House
- ☐ the Gold Coast: go scuba diving
- ☑ Darwin: tour crocodile farm
- ☐ Uluru: climb the rock
- ☐ Perth: try surfing

2 Correct the false statements about Fidel and Paco.

1. Paco hasn't been to Tasmania yet.

   Paco has already been to Tasmania.

2. Fidel and Paco have already visited Perth.

   _____

3. They have already gone scuba diving.

   _____

4. Fidel hasn't been to Darwin yet.

   _____

5. Paco and Fidel haven't been to Melbourne yet.

   _____

6. Fidel has already tried surfing.

   _____

7. Fidel and Paco have already been to Uluru.

   _____

8. Paco hasn't seen the Sydney Opera House yet.

   _____

Lesson 29 In the spotlight

1 Complete the conversation with tag questions.

Mrs. Nelson Hello. You're in my math class this year, _____aren't you_____ ?

Curtis Uh, no, I'm not. I'm in Mrs. Smith's class.

Mrs. Nelson Really? But you took her class two years ago, _____ ?

Curtis No, I didn't.

Mrs. Nelson But she's taught tenth-grade math for a long time, _____ ?

Curtis Yes, she has. But I've never taken her class before.

Mrs. Nelson But you've been a student here since sixth grade, _____ ?

Curtis Yes, I have . . .

Mrs. Nelson And you've finished ninth grade, _____ ?

Curtis Yes, I have. I'm in tenth grade now.

Mrs. Nelson Wait a minute. Are you Chris Wilson?

Curtis No, I'm not. I'm his younger brother, Curtis!

Mrs. Nelson Oh. I'm sorry. Then Chris is in my class, and so is your cousin, Emma. They've always been good at math, _____ ?

2 Write tag questions. Then answer them with your own information.

1. you / be a student / at this school / three years

   Q: _You've been a student at this school for three years,_ **A:** _Yes, I have._
   haven't you?

2. last summer / be very hot

   Q: _____ **A:** _____

3. you / pass sixth-grade math

   Q: _____ **A:** _____

4. your classmates / always be / good students

   Q: _____ **A:** _____

5. soccer / be a popular sport in Brazil / long time

   Q: _____ **A:** _____

6. your friends / live in this town / since they were born

   Q: _____ **A:** _____

7. you / speak English / five years

   Q: _____ **A:** _____

8. your English teacher / give / a lot of homework

   Q: _____ **A:** _____

Lesson
30 Connections

1 Amber Mills loves sports and taking risks. Complete the article about Amber with affirmative or negative present perfect form of the verbs.

Amber Mills: Teen Skateboarder

Amber Mills has loved sports since she was a little girl. So far, she ___has already tried___ (already try) rock climbing, and she _____ (already go) white-water rafting. She _____ (go) skydiving yet, but she'll probably try it someday. Her favorite sport is skateboarding. She started taking skateboarding lessons two years ago, and she _____ (already win) a competition. Her parents were very proud of her. She _____ (already have) an accident, too. She broke her arm last year, but she _____ (already start) skateboarding again. She _____ (become) famous yet, but she'll probably be a famous skateboarder someday!

2 A reporter interviewed Amber for the article in part 1. Write the reporter's tag questions and Amber's answers.

1. (love sports)

   Q: _You've loved sports since you_
   were a little girl, haven't you?

   A: _Yes, I have._

2. (try rock climbing)

   Q: _____

   _____

   A: _____

3. (start taking skateboarding lessons two years ago)

   Q: _____

   _____

   A: _____

4. (have an accident)

   Q: _____

   _____

   A: _____

5. (start skating again)

   Q: _____

   _____

   A: _____

6. (break arm last year)

   Q: _____

   _____

   A: _____

7. (try skydiving)

   Q: _____

   A: _____

8. (win a competition)

   Q: _____

   A: _____

31 Teen opinions

1 **Complete the sentences with the correct forms of the adjectives.**

1. *13 Going on 30* is ___the best___ (good) movie of the year!

2. My mother's cookies are _____ (good) your mother's cookies.

3. _____ (bad) show on TV is *Tough Times*. I don't like it at all.

4. Mary Ann is a _____ (good) friend. She always talks to me when I feel sad.

5. I don't like watching sports at all. I think watching basketball games is _____ (bad) watching tennis matches. Basketball is so boring.

6. It's a _____ (good) song. I really love it!

7. I don't like this food. It tastes pretty _____ (bad).

8. I think Saturday is _____ (good) day of the week. I can sleep late on Saturdays!

2 **Write sentences with the comparative or superlative form of the adjectives.**

1. (*Harry Potter and the Order of the Phoenix* / good / book in the store)
   Superlative: *Harry Potter and the Order of the Phoenix is the best book in the store.*

2. (your grades / good / my grades)
   Comparative: _____

3. (Gregorio's / have / bad pizza in town)
   Superlative: _____

4. (this radio station / play / good music / other radio station)
   Comparative: _____

5. (gym class / bad / math class)
   Comparative: _____

6. (Monday / bad / day of the week)
   Superlative: _____

7. (cats / good / dogs)
   Comparative: _____

8. (soccer / good / sport to play)
   Superlative: _____

3 **Write sentences with the adjectives and your own information.**

1. (messy) *My room is always messy.*

2. (beautiful) _____

3. (entertaining) _____

4. (awful) _____

5. (difficult) _____

6. (scary) _____

Unit 7 Teen Time

㉜ Unforgettable moments

1 Write the superlative form of the adjectives.

1. disgusting *the most disgusting*
2. thrilling _____
3. difficult _____
4. beautiful _____
5. happy _____

6. short _____
7. funny _____
8. exciting _____
9. young _____
10. unforgettable _____

2 Answer the questions. Use the superlative + *have ever*.

1. **A** Is the movie good?
   B (movie / see) *Yes, it is. It's the best movie I've ever seen!*
2. **A** Is the book you're reading scary?
   B (book / read) _____
3. **A** Is your teacher forgetful?
   B (person / meet) _____
4. **A** Is the homework assignment frustrating?
   B (assignment / do) _____
5. **A** Is your brother's room messy?
   B (room / see) _____
6. **A** Are your classes interesting?
   B (classes / take) _____
7. **A** Is the food at that restaurant bad?
   B (food / eat) _____
8. **A** Is your family's new car big?
   B (car / have) _____

3 Answer the questions with your own information.

1. Who's the tallest person you've ever met? *My uncle is the tallest person I've ever met.*
2. What's the longest book you've ever read? _____
3. What's the scariest movie you've ever seen? _____
4. What's the hardest class you've ever taken? _____
5. Who's the funniest person you've ever met? _____
6. What's the most delicious food you've ever eaten? _____

1 What are these people saying? Look at the pictures, and write sentences.

1. (desk / messy) *Your desk is very messy.*
It's messier than my desk. It's the
messiest desk I've ever seen!

2. (bicycle / nice) _____

_____

3. (pet / scary) _____

_____

_____

4. (printer / fast) _____

_____

_____

2 Look at Damon's list. Then write sentences using the superlative + *have ever*.

difficult sport – skiing
funny movie – School Vacation
bad book – The Long Road
interesting person – Professor Alden
good CD – The Greatest Hits
        Collection by Alan Jackson
beautiful place – Ipanema Beach

1. (sport / try) *Skiing is the most difficult sport he's ever tried.*

2. (book / read) _____

3. (CD / buy) _____

4. (movie / see) _____

5. (person / meet) _____

6. (place / visit) _____

Lesson 33 Are we alike?

1 Write sentences comparing the people and the items.

Jake / Jean / tall / short

1. *Jake isn't as tall as Jean.*

   Jean isn't as short as Jake.

black skirt / white skirt / expensive

2. _____

small car / big car / slow / fast

3. _____

   _____

Shelly / Kelly / happy / sad

4. _____

   _____

2 Read about Ramona's family. Then write sentences using formal comparisons for numbers 1–4 and informal comparisons with object pronouns for numbers 5–8.

I have a twin brother, Ricardo. We look alike: I'm as tall as him, and I'm as athletic as him. Of course, I'm as old as him! Our personalities are similar, too. We're both artistic, but I'm not as artistic as Ricardo. He isn't as outgoing as me. But we're both very funny. We have two younger sisters. They're cute, but they aren't as funny as us! They're really shy. We're not as shy as them.

1. (Ramona / tall / Ricardo) *Ramona is as tall as Ricardo is.*
2. (Ramona / athletic / Ricardo) _____
3. (Ramona / artistic / Ricardo) _____
4. (the sisters / old / Ricardo and Ramona) _____
5. (Ricardo / outgoing / Ramona) *He isn't as outgoing as her.*
6. (Ramona / funny / Ricardo) _____
7. (Ramona / old / Ricardo) _____
8. (Ramona / shy / her sisters) _____

Lesson 34 I'd rather . . .

1 Look at the pictures. Then write sentences.

1. (Lucia / take piano lessons / dance lessons)
   Lucia would rather take dance lessons
   than piano lessons.

2. (Pete and Rick / read books / watch TV)
   _____
   _____

3. (Justin / play soccer / play chess)
   _____
   _____

4. (Katie / eat fruit / eat ice cream)
   _____
   _____

5. (Linda / meet a movie star / meet a
   sports star)
   _____
   _____

6. (Paul / stay home / go out)
   _____
   _____

2 Write questions with the verb phrases in the box. Then answer them with your own information.

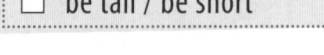

☐ be funny / be artistic   ☑ buy a radio / buy a CD player
☐ be tall / be short   ☐ explore an old house / explore a cave

1. **Q:** _Would you rather buy a radio or a CD player?_
   A: _I'd rather buy a CD player._

2. **Q:** _____
   A: _____

3. **Q:** _____
   A: _____

4. **Q:** _____
   A: _____

Lesson 35 Connections

1 Look at the items in the catalog. Write sentences about the items that you would prefer to buy and why.

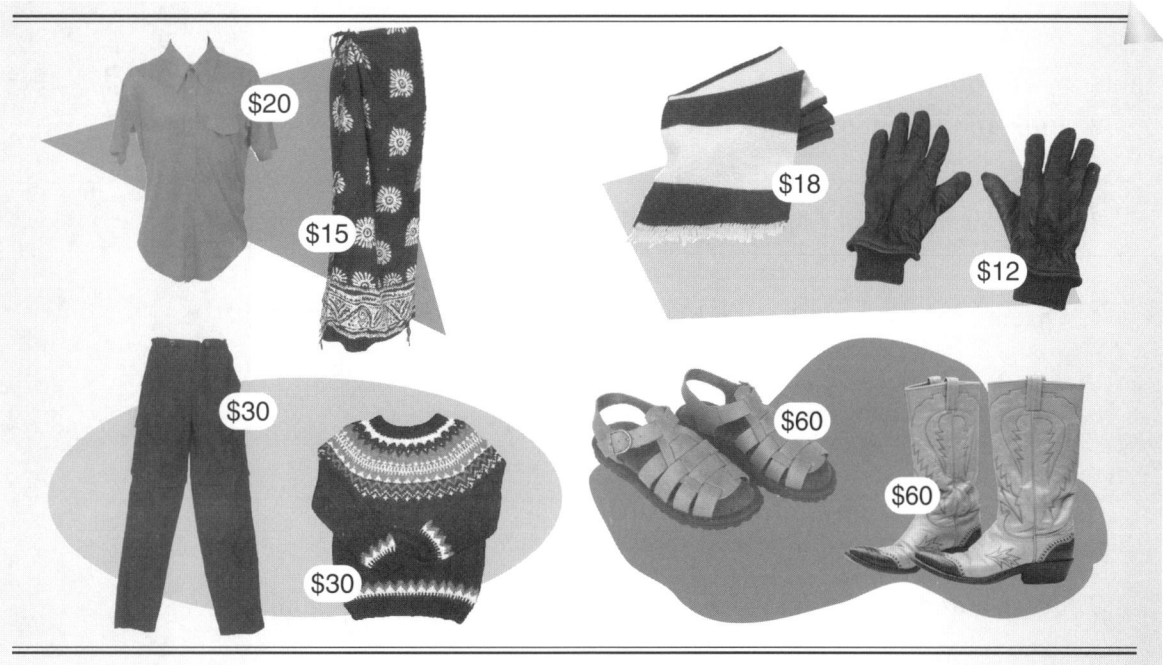

1. *I'd rather buy the skirt than the shirt.*
   The skirt isn't as expensive as the shirt.

2. _____
   _____

3. _____
   _____

4. _____
   _____

2 Write questions and answers.

1. **Q:** *Would Henry rather go to Alaska or Ecuador?*
   A: Henry would rather to go Ecuador than Alaska.

2. **Q:** _____
   A: Mr. Mason would rather buy a bicycle than a motorcycle.

3. **Q:** _____
   A: Brittany would rather read a magazine than watch a movie.

4. **Q:** Would you rather have a pet cat or a pet dog?
   A: (dog) _____

5. **Q:** Would Al and Phil rather learn to play the guitar or the violin?
   A: (violin) _____

6. **Q:** Would you rather watch a soccer match or play soccer?
   A: (play soccer) _____

1 Write sentences.

1. Maria / take a trip next summer / Belize
   If Maria could take a trip next summer, she'd take a
   trip to Belize.

2. Luis and Renaldo / watch any movie / *Spirited Away*
   _____

3. Marissa and Eliot / join a new club / the Photography Club
   _____

4. Gisela / buy new clothes / a black dress
   _____

5. my sister / learn a new sport / snowboarding
   _____

6. we / be good at any activity / painting
   _____

7. Jessica and Aileen / have any kind of dessert / chocolate cake
   _____

8. we / live in any city / San Juan
   _____

2 Complete the sentences.

1. *If I could visit any country*, I'd visit Japan.
2. _____, I'd try bowling.
3. _____, I'd talk to George W. Bush.
4. _____, I'd get a dog.
5. _____, I'd buy the new Rolling Stones CD.
6. _____, I'd be good at tennis.
7. _____, I'd look like Tom Cruise.

3 Look at part 2. Rewrite the sentences with your own information.

If I could visit any country, I'd visit Italy.

1. _____
2. _____
3. _____
4. _____
5. _____
6. _____
7. _____

Lesson 37 What would you do?

1 **Complete the sentences.**

1. If Carrie won a lot of money, _she'd give_ (give) it to charity.
2. What _____ (you / do) if you found a lost dog?
3. If you broke your promise, _____ (I / be) very angry.
4. What _____ (Lana / do) if she _____ (not pass) her test?
5. If I _____ (lose) this camera, I _____ (not buy) a new one.

2 **Complete the sentences with the sentences in the box.**

☐ I'd lend it to him ☐ I'd take it to the Lost and Found
☑ I'd put the garbage in the trash can ☐ I wouldn't litter. I'd throw it in the trash can

1. If I saw someone litter, _I'd put the garbage in the trash can_ .
2. If I found an expensive bracelet in the school bathroom, _____ .
3. If I had some garbage, _____ .
4. If my friend needed to borrow some money, _____ .

3 **Write questions. Then match the questions to the answers.**

1. your friend / ask you to trespass
   What would you do if your friend   e
   asked you to trespass?

2. your friend / want to gossip
   _____ __
   _____

3. your sister / break a promise to you
   _____ __
   _____

4. you see someone / shoplifting
   _____ __
   _____

5. you see someone / eavesdropping on
   your conversation
   _____ __
   _____

6. your classmate / ask you to cheat on a test
   _____ __
   _____

a. I'd be angry. Breaking promises
   is really awful.

b. I'd tell him to gossip with
   someone else.

c. I'd move to another place to talk.

d. I'd say no. The teacher would
   fail both of us.

e. I'd refuse. Trespassing is
   dangerous.

f. I'd tell the store manager.

Dreams and Reality 45

1 Write sentences with *if* clauses and *could*.

1. (he / go / moon)

   If he could go anywhere, he'd go to
   the moon.

2. (Carolyn / meet / Liv Tyler)

   _____

   _____

3. (Andy and Ann / buy / airplane)

   _____

   _____

4. (Romeo / try / sumo wrestling)

   _____

   _____

2 Write questions. Then answer the questions with your own information.

1. (find an expensive ring)

   Q: *What would you do if you found an expensive ring?*

   A: *If I found an expensive ring, I'd try to find the owner.*

2. (lose your English book)

   Q: _____

   A: _____

3. (see someone shoplifting)

   Q: _____

   A: _____

4. (your brother lie to you)

   Q: _____

   A: _____

5. (fail a test)

   Q: _____

   A: _____

6. (meet a famous person)

   Q: _____

   A: _____

Lesson 38 What I'm going to be

1 Circle the two jobs that best match each description.

1. A person who asks many questions   (detective)   carpenter   (scientist)
2. A person who flies in a vehicle   astronaut   pilot   author
3. A person who likes adventure   detective   veterinarian   astronaut
4. A person who makes things   astronaut   artist   carpenter
5. A person who writes a lot   journalist   author   computer programmer

2 Write sentences with infinitives to give a reason.

1. Linda is going to work with children.

   (teacher) _Linda is going to be a teacher to work with children._

2. Michael wants to paint pictures.

   (artist) _____

3. Carlita is going to work with animals.

   (veterinarian) _____

4. I want to build furniture.

   (carpenter) _____

5. Will is going to teach martial arts.

   (karate instructor) _____

6. Sarah and Jocelyn would like to travel to outer space.

   (astronauts) _____

7. Carmen is going to write funny stories for children.

   (author) _____

8. My best friend and I want to work with the latest technology.

   (computer programmers) _____

3 Answer the questions with the phrases in the box.

☐ make discoveries	☐ star in movies
☑ report on events and write articles	☐ travel to interesting places
☐ solve mysteries	☐ write stories

1. Why are you going to be a journalist? _I'm going to be a journalist to report on events_
   and write articles.

2. Why is Carol going to be a detective? _____

3. Why does your sister want to be a pilot? _____

4. Why would Hector like to be an actor? _____

5. Why are you and Amalia going to be authors? _____

6. Why do Camille and Chloe want to be scientists? _____

Dreams and Reality 47

Lesson 39 The past year

1 Choose the correct words to complete the sentences.

1. I can't think of _anything_ (anything / something) to do today.

2. My uncle is _____ (anyone / someone) I admire.

3. I haven't met _____ (anyone / someone) famous.

4. I don't want to go _____ (anywhere / somewhere) this weekend.

5. Tom went _____ (anywhere / somewhere) really cool last weekend.

6. My teacher said _____ (anything / something) that I don't understand.

2 Complete the conversation with *anyone, anything, anywhere, someone, something,* or *somewhere*.

Carmen Hi, Liza. What are you doing here?

Liza I'm looking for a birthday present for __someone__.

Carmen Oh? Is the present for _____ I know?

Liza Well, . . . it's for Eric, my boyfriend.

Carmen I see! It's for _____ special. What are you going to buy?

Liza I don't know! I can't think of _____ he likes.

Carmen He likes sports. Buy him _____ he can use when he plays sports. How about a helmet?

Liza A helmet? I can't buy him _____ like that! That's too weird.

Carmen OK. Then buy him a gift certificate for a restaurant. Then he can take you _____ nice.

Liza Good idea! Can you think of _____ I can go to buy one?

3 Write questions. Then answer them with your own information.

1. meet someone special / this year

   Q: _Have you met anyone special this year?_

   A: _Yes. I met someone at the beach._ OR
   No, I haven't met anyone special this year.

2. go somewhere new / last week

   Q: _____

   A: _____

3. have / do something fun / this month

   Q: _____

   A: _____

4. there is something new / on TV / tonight

   Q: _____

   A: _____

5. give someone a present / last month

   Q: _____

   A: _____

6. eat somewhere special / last month

   Q: _____

   A: _____

Lesson 40 Connections

1 Complete the texts with *anyone, anything, anywhere, someone,* *something*, or *somewhere*.

1. Hi! I'm Hayley. I want to do _something_ special in the future. I don't want to do _____ boring. I'm going be a pilot to travel _____ interesting and meet new people. But I don't want to travel _____ that's very cold!

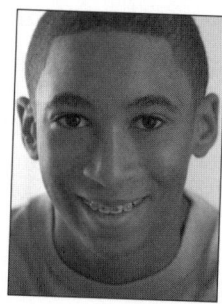
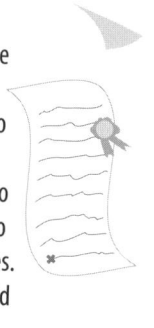

2. My name's Jared. I love solving puzzles and mysteries, so I want to do _____ that makes me think. I want to be _____ who finds answers to mysteries. If I could be a detective, I'd be really happy!

3. Hello, I'm Joe. I'm _____ who loves animals. I'm going to be a veterinarian. I also love the water, so I want to help animals that live in the water. I want to go _____ to study animals.

4. I'm Kristen. I've never met _____ who has the job I want: an author. An author is _____ who writes stories. I'm going to be an author to write interesting stories and books. I like funny stories, so I don't want to write _____ that's too serious!

2 Complete the sentences with information from part 1. For numbers 5 and 6, write about yourself and your best friend.

1. Kristen _is going to be_ an author _to write interesting stories and books_ .

2. Joe _____ a veterinarian _____ .

3. Jared _____ a detective _____ .

4. Hayley _____ a pilot _____ .

5. I _____ .

6. My best friend _____ .

3 Write statements with your own information.

(somewhere) _I went somewhere interesting this week. I_ _went to a museum._

1. (someone) _____

2. (anywhere) _____

3. (anything) _____

4. (something) _____

5. (somewhere) _____

6. (anyone) _____

Check Yourself-Unit 1

A Complete the sentences with the simple past or the past continuous.

1. We _were walking_ (walk) in the park when we ___met___ (meet) some friends.
2. When he _____ (be) a child, Martin _____ (take) piano lessons.
3. When it _____ (start) to rain, the children _____ (play) outside.
4. I was _____ (think) about you when you _____ (call)!
5. Kelly _____ (break) her arm when she _____ (play) volleyball.
6. When I _____ (be) five years old, I _____ (start) school.

B How did Springfield change? Look at the information. Then write sentences.

Springfield in 1956   Springfield now

- small town   - quiet   - city   - noisy
- had a lot of trees - had a lot of bicycles - has a shopping mall - has a lot of cars

1. _Springfield used to be a small town, but it isn't anymore. Now it's a city._
2. _____
3. _____
4. _____

C Write sentences about hopes and wishes, obligations, or definite plans.

1. Liz / work in a record store / next summer

   (definite plan) _Liz is going to work in a record store next summer._

2. I / do English and math homework / tonight

   (obligation) _____

3. we / join a new club / in September

   (hope) _____

4. my classmates / go to college / next year

   (definite plan) _____

5. Jorge / play soccer in the park / this weekend

   (wish) _____

Check Yourself - Unit 2

A Look at the predictions about cars in the future. Then write sentences.

| **Cars in the future** | ✓ = will happen |
| ✖ use gasoline ✓ be small ✓ fly in the sky ✓ go very fast ✖ have wheels | ✖ = won't happen |

1. _Cars won't use gasoline._
2. _____
3. _____
4. _____
5. _____

B Complete the conversations. Write sentences with *will, won't, might,* or *might not.*

1. **A** Are you feeling OK?

   B No, I'm not. I feel awful. (go to school today) _I won't go to school today._

2. **A** Are your neighbors going on vacation?

   B They're not sure. (go to Costa Rica) _____

3. **A** Are you going to go to the mall with us this afternoon?

   B I don't know. I'm really tired. (go with you) _____

4. **A** Are you going to walk to the park?

   B No, I'm not. It's very far away. (ride my bike) _____

5. **A** What are you going to do your report on?

   B I like famous explorers and I know a lot about them.

   (write about Magellan) _____

6. **A** Are you going to join the talent show?

   B Yes, I am. I'm not sure what I'll do. (play the guitar or sing) _____

7. **A** Did you hear about Justin? He broke his leg yesterday!

   B Yes, I heard about him. (be at soccer practice today) _____

C Answer the questions.

1. Will Evan watch TV tonight? (no / probably) _No. He probably won't watch TV tonight._
2. Is Amy going to the concert? (yes) _____
3. Will your parents drive you to my house? (yes / probably) _____
4. Will you do your homework on Friday night? (no) _____
5. Will it rain tomorrow? (no / probably) _____
6. Will you go to college? (yes) _____
7. Will Carla buy a CD today? (yes / might) _____
8. Are your parents going to go to Rio de Janeiro next year? (no) _____

Check Yourself-Unit 3

A **Write questions. Then write acceptances or refusals.**

1. invitation: play tennis with me today

   Q: _Would you like to play tennis with me today?_

   A: (refuse) _I'm sorry, but I can't. I hurt my arm._

2. request: lend me $10

   Q: _____

   A: (refuse) _____

3. permission: stay out late tonight

   Q: _____

   A: (accept) _____

4. invitation: come over tonight

   Q: _____

   A: (accept) _____

B **Match the verb phrases to the clauses. Then use them to write sentences with *if*.**

1. it snows _d_   a. not eat lunch

2. it's sunny _____   b. go to sleep

3. I'm not hungry _____   c. go to the beach

4. I'm exhausted _____   d. go skiing

1. (probably) _If it snows, I'll probably go skiing._

2. (might) _____

3. (will) _____

4. (probably) _____

C **Read Jay's notes about his ski vacation. Then write sentences with *before*, *while*, or *after*.**

> First, I'm going to find my skis. I think they're in the garage. Then I have to buy new gloves and a new hat. I can buy them at the same time. On vacation, I'm going to take skiing lessons. I'm going to make friends with the other kids who are taking lessons. When I get back, I have to write a report for school. But first, I'm going to call my friends!

1. find his skis / go on vacation   _He's going to find his skis before he goes on vacation._

2. buy new gloves / buy a hat _____

3. take skiing lessons / find his skis _____

4. meet new friends / take skiing lessons _____

5. write a report for school / get home _____

6. call all his friends / write a report for school _____

Check Yourself - Unit 4

A Write tag questions. Use gerunds as subjects or objects. Then write the answers.

1. Sara / like / dance

   Sara likes dancing, doesn't she? _____ (no) *No, she doesn't.*

2. play chess / difficult

   _____ (yes) _____

3. you / enjoy / go to the movies

   _____ (no) _____

4. send e-mail and chat online / popular

   _____ (yes) _____

5. Kenza and Ali / like / play sports

   _____ (yes) _____

B Look at the pictures. Write sentences with *too* or *either*.

1. *Lucinda is creative.*
   Joe is, too.

2. _____ _____

3. _____ _____

4. _____ _____

C Look at the information. Then write sentences with *who*.

Lance Armstrong	Sammy Sosa	Jennifer Garner	Shakira
cyclist	baseball player	actor	Colombian singer
has three children	plays for the Chicago Cubs	likes kickboxing	sings in English and Spanish

1. *Lance Armstrong is a cyclist who has three children.*

2. _____

3. _____

4. _____

Check Yourself - Unit 5

A Write questions and answers with the present perfect.

1. **A** (you / ever meet a sports star) *Have you ever met a sports star?*

   B (no) *No, I haven't.*

2. **A** (your parents / listen to your CDs) _____

   B (yes) _____

3. **A** (you / be busy / this month) _____

   B (yes) _____

4. **A** (you / buy any new clothes / this week) _____

   B (no) _____

5. **A** (Luis and Ramon / ever join a fan club) _____

   B (yes) _____

B Dennis and Fernando are musicians. Look at the information. Then write sentences about what they have done (✓) and have not done (✘).

1. *Dennis has written songs.*
2. _____
3. _____
4. _____
5. _____
6. _____
7. _____
8. _____

DENNIS	**FERNANDO**
✓ WRITE SONGS	✓ PLAY THE GUITAR
✘ PLAY THE GUITAR	✓ PLAY AT A CLUB
✘ RECORD A SONG	✘ PLAY WITH A BAND
✓ ENTERTAIN A LIVE AUDIENCE	✓ WIN A TALENT COMPETITION

C Write questions and long answers.

1. you / be a student at this school / September

   Q: *How long have you been a student at this school?*

   A: *I've been a student at this school since September.*

2. Alicia / live here / three months

   Q: _____

   A: _____

3. your parents / have their car / a year

   Q: _____

   A: _____

4. Tomás and Sarah / be Madonna fans / 1985

   Q: _____

   A: _____

Check Yourself - Unit 6

A Choose the correct words to complete the sentences.

1. I studied art _____*for*_____ (for / since) two weeks last summer.

2. Our last concert was two months _____ (since / ago).

3. They've _____ (already / yet) finished their science projects.

4. I haven't gone shopping _____ (so far / since) last weekend.

5. We haven't found summer jobs _____ (already / yet).

6. Laura has done very well in class _____ (so far / ago).

7. I've learned a lot of new English words _____ (ago / so far) this year.

8. Danny has _____ (yet / already) cleaned his room.

B Complete the interview with tag questions and answers.

Reporter Hello, Charlie. I'm going to ask you some questions. _*You've been*_ (you / be) a violinist since you were about six years old, _*haven't you*_ ?

Charlie Yes, _____ .

Reporter Your parents _____ (buy) you your first violin a long time ago, _____ ?

Charlie No, _____ . My brother bought it for me. He's a great brother.

Reporter _____ (you / entertain a live audience) for the first time when you were 11, _____ ?

Charlie Yes, _____ . I was very proud!

Reporter And since then, _____ (you / play) in many countries, _____ ?

Charlie No, _____ . I've never performed outside the U.S.!

C Write present perfect questions with *ever*. Then write answers with *never*.

1. **Q:** (you / travel to England) _*Have you ever traveled to England?*_
   A: _*No, I haven't. I've never traveled to England.*_ OR _*No, never.*_

2. **Q:** (Maria / go to a rain forest) _____
   A: _____

3. **Q:** (you / dye your hair) _____
   A: _____

4. **Q:** (John / try rock climbing) _____
   A: _____

5. **Q:** (Jen and Ron / win a marathon) _____
   A: _____

6. **Q:** (Martina / meet a famous person) _____
   A: _____

Check Yourself–Unit 7

A Write questions and answers.

1. have a cat / have a dog

   Q: _Would you rather have a cat or a dog?_

   A: (cat / cute) _I'd rather have a cat than a dog. Cats are cuter than dogs._

2. study German / study Italian

   Q: _____

   A: (Italian / difficult) _____

3. watch *Monsters* / watch *The Haunted Cave*

   Q: _____

   A: (*The Haunted Cave* / scary) _____

4. eat at Bono's Burgers / eat at The Golden Palace

   Q: _____

   A: (The Golden Palace / better food) _____

B Look at the information. Compare the items using formal and informal comparisons.

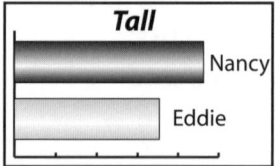 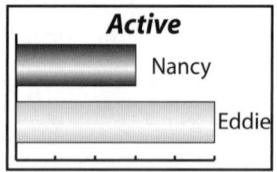 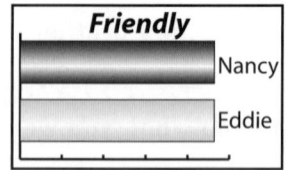

1. (tall) _Eddie isn't as tall as Nancy._
   Eddie isn't as tall as her.

2. (active) _____

   _____

3. (friendly) _____

   _____

4. (artistic) _____

   _____

C Complete the text with the superlative forms of the words + *have ever*.

If you want to go on a great vacation, go to the Rolling River Ranch. It's
_the best place I've ever visited_____ (good place / visit)! I went horseback riding for the
first time there. Horseback riding is _____ (hard sport / try),
but I liked it. The horses there were _____ (big horses / see).
I only fell off once – when I saw a cute boy. That is _____
(embarrassing experience / have). But it was OK. He didn't laugh, and we became friends.
He is _____ (nice boy / meet). Too bad he doesn't live in my
town! But he sends me _____ (long e-mails / read). Maybe
we'll meet again when I go back to the ranch next year.

Check Yourself - Unit 8

A What are Missy's dreams? Write sentences.

My Dreams
travel to Brazil   meet Gwyneth Paltrow
get a CD player   study computer science

1. (travel to any country) _If Missy could travel to any country, she'd travel to Brazil._

2. (get any gift) _____

3. (meet any movie star) _____

4. (study any subject) _____

B Write sentences about Missy's reasons for her choices. Use the information from part A and the verb phrases in the box.

☐ get an autograph   ☐ learn to design Web sites   ☐ listen to music   ☑ see the rain forests

1. _She's going to travel to Brazil to see the rain forests._

2. _____

3. _____

4. _____

C Complete the sentences with *anyone, anything, anywhere, someone, something,* or *somewhere.*

1. Did you do ____anything____ special last weekend?

2. I'm going to meet _____ special tonight – my girlfriend.

3. I did _____ interesting this month. I built my own computer!

4. I can't think of _____ else to invite to my party.

5. I want to go _____ warm this winter.

6. They didn't go _____ last summer.

D Complete the questions and answers with the correct conditional form of the verbs.

1. **Q:** What _would you do_ (you / do) _if you won_ (you / win) a lot of money?

   A: _If I won a lot of money, I'd take a trip_ (take a trip) somewhere.

2. **Q:** What _____ (your parents / do) _____ (you / stay out late)?

   A: _____ (they / be) angry.

3. **Q:** What _____ (your sister / do) _____ (you / go) into her room without permission?

   A: _____ (she / tell) my parents.

Illustration Credits

Laurie Conley 2, 18

Chuck Gonzales 15, 23, 28, 40, 41, 51

Adam Hurwitz 33, 35

Jon Keegan 4, 18, 22, 27, 39, 42, 49, 50

Ben Shannon 8, 32, 53

Photographic Credits

3 ©Steve Raymer/Corbis

6 ©Creatas

7 ©Ryan McVay/Getty Images

9 ©Alamy

10 ©Alamy

12 *(left to right)* ©Getty Images; ©Ariel Skelly/Corbis

13 ©Getty Images

16 ©Stephen Welstead/Corbis

17 ©Stanley Rowan/IndexStock

14 ©Tomas del Amo/IndexStock

16 ©Mike Robinson/SuperStock

19 ©Nicolas Russel/Getty Images

20 ©Creatas

22 ©Getty Images

24 *(clockwise from top left)* ©Corbis; ©Tom Stewart/Corbis; ©Michael DeYoung/Corbis; ©David Young-Wolff/Photo Edit; ©Creatas; ©Mark Peterson/Corbis

25 *(clockwise from top right)* ©Richard Carson/ Reuters/Corbis; ©Corbis; ©Corbis; ©David Kelly Crow/Photo Edit; ©Jose Luis Pelaez, Inc/Corbis; ©Corbis; ©David Young-Wolff/Photo Edit

26 ©Corbis

29 ©Mary Kate Denny/Photo Edit

30 ©Joe Feingersh/Corbis

31 *(top to bottom)* ©Getty Images; ©Warner Bros./Getty Images

34 ©Stephen Simpson/Getty Images

35 ©Sergio Pitamitz/Alamy

37 ©Corbis

38 *(top to bottom)* ©Corbis; ©Richard Hutchings/Corbis

42 ©Rob Lewine/Corbis

43 *(bottom)* ©Alfredo Marquiez/LonelyPlanet

44 *(top to botoom)* ©Angelo Cavalli/SuperStock; ©Getty Images

46 *(clockwise from top left)* ©Arthur Morris/Corbis; ©Scott Gries/Getty Images; ©Pictor International/Alamy; ©Mike Fuller Group/Superstock

47 ©David Pollack/Corbis

48 ©Corbis

49 *(clockwise from top left)* ©David Young-Wolff/Photo Edit; ©George Disario/Corbis; ©Mike Robinson/SuperStock; ©Fotosearch

52 ©Spencer Grant/Photo Edit

54 ©Thinkstock/SuperStock

55 ©Denise DeLuise/Imagestate

Notes

Notes

Notes

Notes